Are you like me?

Bobbie Kalman

🌳 **Crabtree Publishing Company**
www.crabtreebooks.com

Created by Bobbie Kalman

Author and Editor-in-Chief
Bobbie Kalman

Reading consultant
Elaine Hurst

Editors
Kathy Middleton
Crystal Sikkens

Design
Bobbie Kalman
Katherine Berti

Photo research
Bobbie Kalman

Production coordinator and Prepress technician
Katherine Berti

Photographs
Istockphoto: page 4
Other photographs by Shutterstock

Library and Archives Canada Cataloguing in Publication

Kalman, Bobbie, 1947-
    Are you like me? / Bobbie Kalman.

(My world)
ISBN 978-0-7787-9508-7 (bound).--ISBN 978-0-7787-9533-9 (pbk.)

    1. Individual differences--Juvenile literature. I. Title. II. Series:
My world (St. Catharines, Ont.)

BF697.K34 2011   j155.2'2   C2010-901974-1

Library of Congress Cataloging-in-Publication Data

Kalman, Bobbie.
  Are you like me? / Bobbie Kalman.
    p. cm. -- (My world)
  ISBN 978-0-7787-9533-9 (pbk. : alk. paper) -- ISBN 978-0-7787-9508-7
(reinforced library binding : alk. paper)
  1. Individual differences--Juvenile literature. 2. Individual differences in
children--Juvenile literature. I. Title. II. Series.

  BF697.K287 2011
  155.2'2--dc22
                                                          2010011301

Crabtree Publishing Company

www.crabtreebooks.com   1-800-387-7650

Printed in China/072010/AP20100226

Published in Canada
Crabtree Publishing
616 Welland Ave.
St. Catharines, Ontario
L2M 5V6

Published in the United States
Crabtree Publishing
PMB 59051
350 Fifth Avenue, 59th Floor
New York, New York 10118

Published in the United Kingdom
Crabtree Publishing
Maritime House
Basin Road North, Hove
BN41 1WR

Published in Australia
Crabtree Publishing
386 Mt. Alexander Rd.
Ascot Vale (Melbourne)
VIC 3032

Words to know

adult   animals   clothes

Earth

living things

people (families)   plant   skateboarding

Are you like me?

Are you a girl, or are you a boy?

Is your face like mine?

Is your hair or skin like mine?

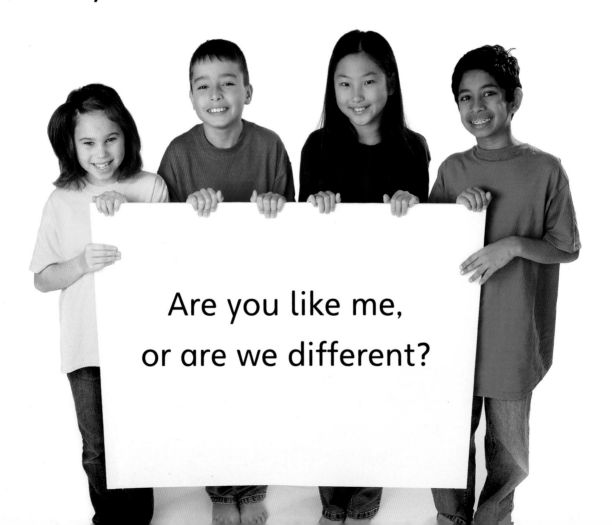

Are you like me,
or are we different?

You are like me in many ways.

We share the same home.

We live on **Earth**.

sunshine

air

water

You are like me because
we are both **living things**.
Living things need sunshine, air, and water.

You and I need food, a home, and **clothes** to wear.
We need **plants** and **animals**.
We need other **people**.

home

plants

people

food

clothes

animal

You and I were babies once.

We are children now.

We will be **adults** when we grow up.

babies

children

adults

When we are adults, we may have children.
Then we will be mothers or fathers.

mother

father

children

You and I are the same
in many ways.
We are also different.
We like to do
different things.

I like to play soccer.

I like
to paint.

You and I are good at different things.

I can do some things very well.

What can you do very well?

Can you
skate well?

Can you
dance well?

Can you
sing well?

Are you
good at
skateboarding?

You and I have different ways of life.

We like to eat different foods.

We dress in different clothes.

We have different **families**.
Do you have a mother
and a father?
How many brothers
or sisters do you have?

You are like me in many ways.

You are also different in many ways.

Different is fun!

There is no one
just like me.
I'm the best
that I can be.
I'm so happy,
oh, so happy,
happy to be me!

Are you happy to be you?

Notes for adults

Objective
- to have children look at the ways that they are the same and different

Accomodations
Read the book *Who am I?* to the children to review with them the different roles they play, such as, boy, girl, student, son, daughter.

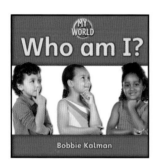

Guided Reading: A

Before reading *Are you like me?*
Ask the children what makes them all the same: What do they need to stay alive? What things do they need to feel safe and happy? How do they all change from the time they are born to the time they become adults?

Class discussion after reading the book
Discuss the ways that people are different. Give the children clues such as gender, name, culture, ways of dressing, and ways they like to have fun. What would it be like if everyone in their family or school were the same? How is being different fun? Ask the children to recite the poem on page 15. Are they happy to be who they are?

Activity: "Tell me all about yourself."
Pair off the children with classmates they do not know well. The partners ask each other questions about: their ages, where they live, their families, and their favorite colors, foods, and activities. When the partners have had enough time to question each other, have the pairs take turns standing in front of the class and telling the other children what they have learned about the child with whom they were paired.

Guided Reading: P

Extensions
Read the book on the left to the children. Ask them to write a poem called "Me from A to Z," like the one mentioned on pages 22-23. For each letter, have the children name a word that describes themselves. Ask them to draw pictures to go with the words.

For teacher's guide, go to www.crabtreebooks.com/teachersguides